Community
Heroes

Selina Li Bi

Heroes are all around us.

They help put out fires.

They help sick people.

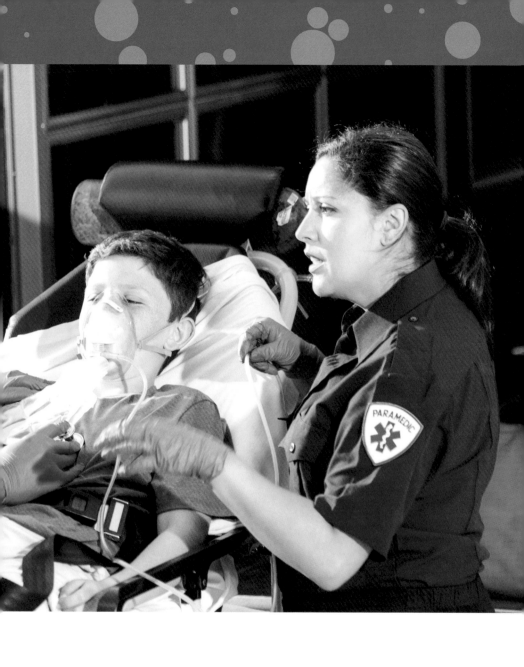

They help bring the
mail.

They help clean up.

They help pets find homes.

They help grow food.

Think and Talk

Where does food come from?

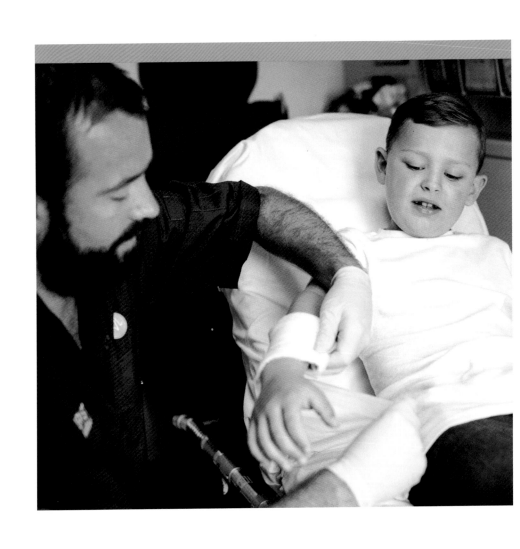

Heroes help us!

Jump into Fiction

Our Food Heroes

They plant seeds.
Plants grow.

They sell food.
The food helps us grow!

Civics in Action

Look around. There are many heroes. They help others.

1. Think of the adults at your school. What jobs do they do? How do they help?

2. Choose one person. Write and draw about them. Show how they help.

3. Show the person what you made. Say thank you!